FOOTPRINTS
IN THE SAND

Reshad Feild's spiritual search has taken
him around the world to Zen monasteries
in Japan, the Himalayas and to Turkey
where he studied the Sufi mystical
traditions and was initiated into the order
of the Mevlevi Dervishes.

He has been in turn a popular singer, an
antique dealer and stockbroker.
Throughout the '70s he ran schools in
human transformation in Britain, Canada
and America. A professional geomancer,
Reshad was granted his doctorate in
psychological counselling in 1983. He is the
author of several other books which have
been described as classics of contemporary
spiritual literature.

FOOTPRINTS IN THE SAND

Originating from
Reshad Feild

and developed by
Matthew Shoemaker

ELEMENT BOOKS

© Reshad T. Feild and Matthew Shoemaker 1988

First published 1988 by
Element Books Limited
Longmead, Shaftesbury, Dorset

Printed and bound in Great Britain by
Billings, Hylton Road, Worcester

Designed by Max Fairbrother

Front and back cover phtographs:
H.C. Heap/Planet Earth Pictures

British Library Cataloguing in Publication Data
Feild, Reshad
Footprints in the sand.
1. Spirituality - Quotations
I. Title
291.4

ISBN 1-85230-027-2

Introduction

This unique collection of expressions from Reshad Feild will be a challenge for the reader. In the course of teaching a class or even cooking a meal, Reshad often comes out with a statement that either baffles the intellect or sings in the heart. These have been called 'snippets', as though they were snipped out of the air. If you have the privelege to attend a class, you may even here someone say to another, "snip it!"

From the many hundreds of these collected gems, I have grouped and arranged the ones here in this particular way to best benefit the reader. The content speaks for itself, and each line has multiple levels of meaning.

One may use these quotations individually or in groups, as contemplations or themes to work with for a time. There are many ways to read and use this book, and I welcome you to find your own. Take it seriously, but have fun with it. This is a guide book for those who are travelling on the way of knowledge, through the gates of love and on to the path of service in this world.

Many thanks to all those who helped collect these words, especially Penny Feild, Subhana Menis, Nancy Skopin, Lewis Austin, Chris Knab and Tony Stanton. And a very special thanks to Reshad Feild for his knowledge, love and work.

Introducing the second volume

Once again, I am proud to bring you these wise and witty phrases of the heart, from the spontaneous responses of Reshad Feild to questions and 'the need of the moment', diligently snatched with perky ears and swift pens, chosen and arranged here in this beautiful volume for your unusual awakening and bed-side enjoyment.

May this book serve you well on your way. Remember though, 'The sound of the book is the sound of the person who reads it'.

MATTHEW SHOEMAKER

This life is
the only one we have
and therefore the greatest
adventure in the world.

There is no end,
to the search —
unfolding within
the ever-present living moment.

The only purpose of being here
is to be here —

yet a very small percentage of us
ever get here.

We are here to be committed
unconditionally to life.

Breath is life,

so how can we
commit ourselves to life
without being awake to breath?

Each time we re-commit
ourselves to life,
we lose a little something
we don't need

and gain a little something
we do need.

The moment you
give up your life
unconditionally to serving mankind

the need for personal power
goes out of the window —

the law of sinchronicity
enters our lives.

We commit ourselves
to every day,
every day.

Once you are committed
You're in for it.

There is no going back —

only turning again and again
to our true heritage
which is the source
of all life.

You must go on.

There's no point in turning back —
there are too many people
coming on behind you.

Reincarnation exists
until you know
you don't need it.

If the sacred cow of reincarnation
is still giving you influenza,
then you better give it up.

So often we merely drift around,
tossed and turned
by the hazards of fate,

not putting ourselves
in the stream of service
or in the arms of destiny.

If you want to be the master
of your own destiny,

don't do anything haphazardly.

Live life passionately
but not controlled by the passions.

Often when we just
'go with the flow',
not making any decisions,

we have given up our will
to the power of attraction.

When we are tired of living

we cannot walk consciously.

Stay conscious!

. . . or at least wake up!

We are here for a reason —
though we may not know it.

When we understand
the laws of service

we are born afresh each day.

Cause is born
out of necessity.

Some people can't reach
the point of necessity,
let alone perplexity...

A certain type of tension
is useful and creative —

it produces a living fire
to be welcomed.

You can't have everything easily —
creative tension is necessary.

In order to complete
a decision in life
we need to have

commitment, willingness and agreement.

There is no stronger word
than agreement —

without it
nothing could exist.

If we can find out
what is within ourselves
that needs to agree
with our agreement,

then we are a long way down the road.

Learn to say thank you
to whatever experience
you are given.

What you are being offered
is what you need to look at.

Be grateful
that you have some blocks on the road —
without them
there would be no need to work.

Blocks may be seen
as stepping stones
to the Truth.

Make every single aspect
of your being
your friend.

There's nothing wrong
with pain,

it's how we interact
with it that matters.

We are given pain
in order to rise above it.

Pain is like a roller coaster —
let it pass quickly.

Let the useless tension go
by putting loving attention on it.

It will all work out
in the end ...

even if you're constipated!

We are continuously
being given experiences
from which we can learn,

when we understand them —
we do not need
them anymore.

Never judge —
but be very discriminating!

To love
does not mean
we have to accept stupidity...

Real love is not an emotion,
thought or sensation —

for it contains
the power of redemption.

You are the agents of God.

When you know
you are loved,
you can be
an agent for love.

Once we know we are loved,
we can get on with it.

Love is both
active and receptive
at once.

We are servants of Grace
and children in the lap of God.

Give agreement to the love
you have been given.

Know you are loved!

In order to know
we are loved,
we have to be empty
enough to receive love.

When we cease to think,
we might really know
we're loved.

When we are in love,
we are in the womb
of the moment.

If we breathe the rhythm of
The Mother's Breath,

we ourselves are
the presence
of the womb of the moment.

We need to be loved
in order to understand

and we need to be together
in order to help.

The experiment on this planet
is to see if we can live
together.

It is so easy
to just presume love
without making
any conscious effort.

God wants a wedding cake,
but don't cut a piece out
before you give it to Him.

If you can't love
all of God's creatures
then a piece is missing.

See love
without the necessity
of form.

Healing comes
from loving
unconditionally.

Once you hear
the sound of forgiveness,
you can be
the instrument of forgiveness.

If you breathe in the right way
you open up life's possibility.

In every conscious breath
a child is conceived
somewhere in the world.

You breathe in what you need
so that you can breathe out
to the world.

Breath brings the wind
of change into our world.

Breath and the tides of breathing,
bring harmony into a discordant world.

Breath brings hope
and deep inner peace.

Breath sounds the note
of conscious
evolution.

Between the in-breath
and the out-breath

lies the possibility
of the future.

The world of possibility
does not manifest by belief alone.

Visualisation without breath
is like a pen without ink.

Breath contains moisture
so that the world of ideas
can manifest.

If our intention is pure,
it can be directed
to an idea that needs to manifest.

We have to be ready

for an idea
to manifest
through us.

The world of ideas
links up with us
only when we give
agreement to it.

Creative imagination
does not make reality,
but can reflect it.

Visualise with the Light
that God gives you.

Do not fall
into the deadly trap
of expectation.

Expectation kills all possibilities.

Expecting something to be
just the way we want it to be
is just plain bad manners.

The result of such stupidity
is inevitably disappointment,
resentment and grief.

Without taking a chance
you cannot know life.

The way to conquer fear
is to make a decision.

Initiation means taking a step
in a direction that is unknown.

Realise the future
that is coming to you

and time will be
on your side.

To the extent
we give ourselves up
to the Truth itself

there is room for it
to enter into manifestation.

When we really want
the Truth,

it will manifest
in the outer world.

Remember your purpose
on as many levels
as possible.

The purpose of life
is to find the Truth,
to love the Truth,
and to stand by the Truth.

God help you!

The magic word
that opens the door of Truth,
is the sound of the word
of the present moment.

Truth has no dimension,
yet is extended
into dimension,
through time.

Follow the fingerprints
of Truth.

Each individual
has to find his own reality,
but not at the expense of everyone else!

There is nothing wrong
with wishing something
for yourself,

if you understand
it is for everyone else as well.

The wish of God
is that we know
ourself.

Knowing yourself
does not just mean
studying your psychology
or the way your ego ticks,

but is discovered
by a complete dedication to life itself.

It is the only life
we have.

When you have found yourself
you have knowledge —

until then
you only have opinions.

We must keep our 'I am'
out of the way
of the great 'I AM'.

If we really want
to come into unconditional union,
we will certainly be tested.

A woman said to me,
'I'm partially disabled ... '

Well, who isn't?

The more special you feel
the more you have covered up
what you have to face.

We project a mirror reflection
of ourselves onto others —

when we cannot face
in ourselves

what we need
for our own completion.

I am merely a mirror
for people to understand
themselves.

If we are witnesses of God
and God made us in His image,
then we are the mirrors

of His Truth.

You can find
the inner Guide
anywhere.

Nothing is more manifest
nor more hidden than God.

The more we are awake
the less separation there is
between God and ourselves.

To be healed
means to be whole.

To be whole
means that there is
no separation.

There is a state of knowing
that we are not separate
from the Unity.

All healing
is healing from illusion,
so give up your concepts.

In completion
there is nothing left
but God!

The less
there is of you

the more places you can be
in at once.

If you turn inside out,
what is not within?

The soul is
a knowing substance.

The soul knows
because the soul remembers.

The seat of the soul
is in the heart.

The human soul
is the dwelling place
of God.

When we know ourself
we know our existence
has always been
God's existence.

If you do not know
you are important
you are denying God's existence
in this world.

Each one of us
uniquely represents the Unity,
yet we are not separate.

It is misuse of thought
that makes separation.

If we remember
the uniqueness of God,
we will respect
God in each other.

Remember we are all unique,

so beauty is in the eyes
of the beholder.

There is not one thumb-print
that is the same.

You are all uniquely beautiful!

God is within,
waiting to be released
through the knowledge
that indeed we are loved.

God is love!

The imprisoned God within
is freed through recognition,
though often it takes time.

When the time is right
and one is ready,
it only takes a glance
from a conscious human being.

The split second
between the bud
and the rose

is known only by those
who have become roses.

Whenever you look
into someone's eyes,
knowing, 'I love you',

you leave that pattern
on the face of the earth.

When we can see beauty and love
in all of God's creatures
we have Being.

Until then
we are a cloudy mirror.

Address the God in another
with the God within you.

You cannot release
the God in you
without trust
in the present moment.

Every time we allow
ourselves to be seen,
another human being wakes up.

As you recognise
life from the heart
it begins to know itself.

When you recognise the elements
they can come to help you.

Earth energy comes alive
when you recognise it.

Everything we see here
is the manifestation
of an invisible pattern
and a guide to the Real World.

Anyone thinking
only of themselves
will not find the Real world.

We are so limited
by our concepts
of what this world is

that we cannot see
that all the worlds
are within us.

Who we think we are is a product
of the false imagination
of the past.

Attachment and identification
betray the truth
of who you are.

Don't identify
with all your ups and downs —
it's not all of you.

Don't live in the memory pattern
of comparison.

How can we be free
if our life is governed
by the conditioned mind?

The past is redeemed
through the present,
but only when we are present.

Completion comes as fast
as we can let go of the past.

If we don't relax
into the present moment,
we can create hell on earth.

True freedom
lies within the sound
of the present moment.

Surrender your heart
into the present moment.

If you listen
to anything carefully
from your heart,

you will hear the Hū.

The sound of the Hū
is always here,
everywhere,

but it needs strings
for us to hear it.

Attune yourself
to the first manifested sound
of the universe.

If you can hear
the Hū everywhere,
there is no separation.

Capacity is relative
to our degree of emptiness.

Until you die
before you die,
you cannot know
anything about Being,

and there is
no freedom without it.

If you honestly face yourself
in the mirror,
you will face death.

Visualize your death,
then know this is your life.

You don't die
until you live,

and you don't really live
until you die.

Once you have died
to yourself
there is only
the present moment,

and you are born
into Eternity.

Every moment is new
as long as you are awake.

You find life in substance
and you think about life in dreams.

We are mostly water —
water is a conductor of electricity
and thought-form is an electrical impulse.

All of us carry
an immense amount
of unredeemed thought-forms
with us.

One thought-form collects others like it.
Be careful!

Many of us suffer
from thought-hangovers
from day's —
even years before.

If we are breathing properly,
thought-form that is not useful for us
will not become attached to us.

Through breath
we can raise
our own rate of vibration.

Thinking and
Breathing consciously
don't go together.

If I drop into sentimentality
then I am not on top
of the breath,

and have dropped
below my own dignity.

The Real world
is not clouded
by thought-form.

Refine thought.
Let God think through you.

Make your mind
your friend

be wholly thought

through your heart.

Our inner transformation
does have a profound effect
on the world.

Choose with care
what consciousness
prevails within you.

Let the angels occupy
and surround you.

Reach up like trees
and allow the Light
to nurture you.

Turn your back to the Sun
and allow the Light
behind the sun
to go through you
into the waiting world.

Prayer within the One Being
allows love to flow to
where it is needed.

If you pray in Unity
and gratefulness,
you are the prayer itself.

Devotion cannot conform
to set methods —
it is private, personal,
and develops inside of oneself.

Platitudes to and for God
make bad smells in this world.

Breathe for the world
but don't think about it —

maybe it doesn't want your thoughts!

It is possible to wake up
to our responsibility
in being born man and woman,

and to be custodians
to that which gives us life.

It is indeed our own
personal responsibility
to see that we do things
to the best of our ability

and attune to what is needed
at any one moment.

Ask 'May I? Should I? Can I?'

'May I?' is asking permission
from the Highest.

'Should I?' has to do
with the relationship
between action and time.

'Can I?' questions one's own state
and if the action is possible.

There has to be
a sufficient amount of trust
to attune ourselves
to what is needed.

First there has to be trust,
then love, then knowledge.

Make room for trust
with no opinions.

Be so in love
that you are totally
adaptable and responsible.

Whatever you do,
do it saying
'I love you'.

God gave time to you
and you have no time
to stop using it.

Although we may never fully see
the fruits of our labours,

great things often start
in small ways.

The action we make
can leave a memory behind
to act as a living example
of what can be done,

providing hope for others
to find their own way of helping.

Have a good frame —
it's like a good disguise!

Find out what you are best at,
then manifest your dreams.

Put your talents to good use,
then you will have no rubble
on your head when you die.

Remember the law of reciprocity —
we get nothing free
in the relative world.

You may never personally
reap the results
of your own sacrifices —

but someone will.

Nobody is perfect,
but we *can* serve perfection.

If you don't know what to do,
ask God to inform you.

Have the courage
to be an instrument
of the Highest.

If you cannot accept authority,
at least help it.

You're never bored
if you accept authority,
because you'll always
land up with a question.

Sporadic insights are not enough.

In order to be transformed
we must pursue a single question
to its very end.

If we live
in the question
we are living
in conscious evolution.

When you have a question
alive in your heart,

life becomes a song of glory.

Glorify the very fact
that you can be of service.

The further we go
on this path —

the more grateful we are
to be humble.

The sound of gratefulness
makes love possible
on Earth.

The breath
of the mystic
turns the world.